BLAZERS

HORSEPOWER

ATVS

by Mandy R. Marx

Reading Consultant:
Barbara J. Fox
Reading Specialist
North Carolina State University

Capstone
press

Mankato, Minnesota

Blazers is published by Capstone Press,
151 Good Counsel Drive, P.O. Box 669, Mankato, Minnesota 56002.
www.capstonepress.com

Library of Congress Cataloging-in-Publication Data
Marx, Mandy.
    ATVs/by Mandy R. Marx.
    p. cm.—(Blazers. Horsepower)
    Includes bibliographical references and index.
    ISBN-13: 978-0-7368-5473-3
    ISBN-10: 0-7368-5473-8
    1. All terrain vehicles—Juvenile literature. I. Title. II. Series.
TL235.6.M36 2006
629.22'042—dc22   2005019605

Summary: Discusses ATVs, including their many capabilities,
    competitions, and safety.

Editorial Credits
Jenny Marks, editor; Jason Knudson, set designer; Thomas
    Emery, book designer; Jo Miller, photo researcher; Scott
    Thoms, photo editor

Photo Credits
Corbis/Judy Griesedieck, 15; Richard Hamilton Smith, 11, 14
Getty Images/Al Bello, 12, 28–29
Global Entertainment Network Group LLC, 25
Trackside Photo, cover; Byrie Moore, 7; Dave Rivdahl, 20; Fidel
    Gonzales, 5, 17, 22–23; Jim Ober, 6, 26; PJ Springman, 8-9; Tom
    Murotake, 18, 19

The author dedicates this book to her ATV-loving nephew, Cael.

1 2 3 4 5 6 11 10 09 08 07 06

TABLE OF CONTENTS

The Ultimate Challenge.......... 4

Ready for Anything.............. 10

Racing ATVs 16

Riding Safely.................. 24

ATV Diagram 22

Glossary...................... 30

Read More 31

Internet Sites 31

Index 32

THE ULTIMATE CHALLENGE

ATVs roar over bumps and rip through the air. The Baja 1000 is the ultimate relay race for all-terrain vehicles.

Racers face nearly 1,000 miles (1,600 kilometers) of California desert. Fans line the raceway. They watch the teams blaze through sand and battle the heat.

BLAZER FACT

The first Baja 1000 was held in 1967. Today, ATVs, dune buggies, motorcycles, and pickup trucks race at the Baja 1000.

The winning team takes home a cash prize. But the real reward is the pride gained by completing this challenging race.

READY FOR ANYTHING

ATV stands for all-terrain vehicle. These machines are small but strong. ATVs tackle even the toughest trails.

ATV tires are made for rough riding. Soft rubber and big treads help the tires grip any surface, from deep mud to loose gravel.

Tire treads

BLAZER FACT

Riders change their ATV tires
for different riding surfaces.
Tires with thick, blocky
treads are used on trails.

ATVs were designed for having fun. But farmers, ranchers, and police officers use ATVs for work. Their ATVs can go where other vehicles can't.

BLAZER FACT

ATVs make it easy for ranchers to haul food to animals in fields.

RACING ATVS

Racing is one of the most exciting uses for ATVs. Racers speed head-to-head toward the finish line.

Races are held on many types of courses. They range from dirt tracks to cross-country trails. Some races are even held indoors.

BLAZER FACT

In the 1960s, ATVs had six or even eight wheels! They were used on land and in shallow water.

People of all ages race ATVs. Kids as young as 6 compete on small machines.

BLAZER FACT

Women get in on the action too. Angela Moore raced in ESPN's Great Outdoor Games in 2005.

ATV DIAGRAM

Exhaust pipe

Treaded tire

Engine

Handle bars

Shock absorber

RIDING SAFELY

States have laws to keep ATV riders safe. New riders can get free training from the ATV Safety Institute.

Riders wear goggles and a helmet to protect their eyes and head. Long sleeves, gloves, and boots prevent scrapes. Drivers ride hard, but also ride safely.

BLAZER FACT

Three-wheeled ATVs were outlawed in 1988. They rolled too easily.

AT HOME
IN THE MUD!

GLOSSARY

dune buggy (DOON BUHG-ee)—a motor vehicle with large tires for driving through sand

relay race (REE-lay RAYSS)—a team race in which the members of the team take turns racing

terrain (tuh-RAYN)—ground or land

tread (TRED)—a ridge on a tire that makes contact with the road

READ MORE

Budd, E. S. *ATVs.* Sports Machines. Chanhassen, Minn.: Child's World, 2004.

Maurer, Tracy. *ATV Riding.* Radsports Guides. Vero Beach, Fla.: Rourke, 2003.

Savage, Jeff. *ATVs.* Wild Rides! Mankato, Minn.: Capstone Press, 2004.

INTERNET SITES

FactHound offers a safe, fun way to find Internet sites related to this book. All of the sites on FactHound have been researched by our staff.

Here's how:

1. Visit *www.facthound.com*
2. Type in this special code **0736854738** for age-appropriate sites. Or enter a search word related to this book for a more general search.
3. Click on the **Fetch It** button.

FactHound will fetch the best sites for you!

INDEX

3-wheelers, 27
6-wheelers, 19
8-wheelers, 19

ATV Safety Institute, 24

Baja 1000, 4, 6, 7, 8

courses, 18

laws, 24

Moore, Angela, 21

prizes, 8

races, 16, 18, 20

safety, 24, 26

tires, 12, 13
training, 24

work uses, 14

4/19 (48) 6/19